Anita Bell is the b...
cial titles and thr...

For more informa...
loadable stock-wat...
out her webpage a...

www.anitabell.com

National Library of New Zealand
Cataloguing-in-Publication Data

Bell, Anita, 1967- .
Your sharemarket jargon explained / Anita Bell.

ISBN 1-86941-597-3

1. Stock exchanges—Terminology. 2. Stocks—Terminology.
I. Title.

332.64014—dc 21

A Random House book
published by
Random House New Zealand
18 Poland Road, Glenfield, Auckland, New Zealand
www.randomhouse.co.nz

This edition first published 2003

ISBN 1-86941-597-3

Typeset by Midland Typesetters, Victoria, Australia
Printed and bound by Griffin Press

YOUR SHAREMARKET JARGON

EXPLAINED

TRICKS, TRAPS AND INSIDER HINTS

ANITA BELL

RANDOM HOUSE
NEW ZEALAND

Acknowledgements

To Carol Davidson, good coffee and
meandering conversation on a warm summer's eve
by the banks of the Brisbane River.

Introduction for the sceptical and uninitiated

Are you sick of feeling like the odd yuppie out at the party? Are you scared of the stockmarket? Or do you ever get the feeling that following the herd of investors is leading you to the financial slaughter yards?

Fear not! A few hours inside the pages of this pocket guide will arm you with the terminology, tricks, traps and insider investor info you need to turn fear into fun, losses into profits and reservations into confidence. This book provides the fundamental core of info you need to get you going with ordinary shares. It's the book I wish I'd had when I started out – no nonsense, no information-overload. Just straight to the gist of it, cutting through all the current techno-jargon, simplifying it, and helping you to figure out most of the new terminologies as they crop up.

I hope you'll soon realise that investing in ordinary shares is a truckload less complicated than many

---

Work it out for yourself

Would investment advisors who earn their livelihoods from your wallet prefer to:

a) point you in the direction of free knowledge to help you do things for yourself

b) mystify the industry so you'll prefer to pay them to take care of your portfolio for you

c) sell you complicated and expensive software or subscriptions up to $22,000 each?

---

investment advisors would prefer you to believe. In fact, it can be exciting and fun. So quit putting the topic into your too-hard basket. Join the investors who are making great returns with little effort – in my case using as little as 20 hours a year to manage my portfolio.

And no, it's not betting. As a conservative investor, I've stuck mainly to the safest tips for ordinary shares, rather than going too deeply into the riskier and more complicated lingo behind futures, warrants and options etc., which shouldn't be the domain of the L-plate investor anyway. But with this book, it won't be long before you're sporting a fresh and fuller vocabulary that will also save you from feeling powerless or naive the next time you sit down to plan or tweak your financial future with your bank manager, broker or investment advisor.

I recommend you read the book once from start to finish to begin with, then beginners need only to glance through the underlined bold terms just before they speak with their brokers. The most common terms will then be fresh in your mind. You'll not only understand more of what they're on about, you'll also assist a reputable broker to make more informed and tailored recommendations for you to approve.

Added bonus: you might even impress your friends with your new depth of knowledge! To kick-start your fun sooner, invite them round to your place with a few bottles of your favourite and take your crash-course in the sharemarket together. Just start with a toast from me for your future:

May knowledge, not greed, become the cornerstone to future wealth.

NOTES

1. The most important definitions for L-plate investors – even if you intend to rely on fund managers to make all your investment decisions from now until you die – are in bold and underlined for your convenience.

2. If you see a word(s) in bold and italics, it means this word or phrase is explained elsewhere in alphabetical order, with greater detail.

Warning

If your investment specialist uses more than one term during the course of your first five conversations with them which is/are not mentioned in this book, then you can be fairly certain that either:

a) you're starting at a riskier or more controversial end of the financial pond
b) they're testing your knowledge and/or how much they can get away with
c) they made it up or bastardised an existing term to make it sound like they're on the cutting edge of the industry

If this happens to you, then be suspicious, be veeery suspicious — and feel confident that you can ask them what they mean, safe in the knowledge that you're not going to sound like a naive novice. Be an informed novice instead.

Alphabetical listing

The jargon below is explained alphabetically. It's more than a dictionary of terms, however. This book, like my others, is designed to be read cover to cover in an hour or so. Once again, you'll find cross-references to avoid repeating myself, but also greater definition at the beginning of the book to get you going.

ANNUAL GENERAL MEETING (AGM): A shareholder get-together once a year to drink wine, eat hors d'oeuvres, check out the company's progress, sack or re-elect directors and vote on key matters essential to the running of the company – hopefully before they've consumed too much of the wine. Beware the company whose AGM is held in a difficult location, with little or no parking, accommodation, public transport or seating. If it's deliberately hard for you to get to then chances are the directors want you to stay away, while their chairperson gets to vote on sly issues as your default proxy, with even greater powers if you forget to send in your postal ballot.

ANNUAL REPORT: The booklet produced prior to the Annual General Meeting which includes performance reports, directors' reports, income and expense figures, dividend details (if any), goal plan for the future (or lack thereof) and auditor's report, all of which may be discussed and voted on during the AGM. Some companies are reducing the magazine quality of their annual reports in a responsible attempt to cut costs for shareholders. Use the annual report as your minimum once-a-year check up on each long-term company investment.

ASK: The price someone is 'asking' for their shares. If it's 20% or more than the current selling price, it should be called 'dreaming'.

ASSETS: Everything that a company (or person) owns or has owing to it. Investments, cash, money due, stock and materials are current assets. Machinery and buildings are fixed assets. Goodwill, patents, handshake deals and promises are intangible assets. To figure out *net assets*, you just total all the assets and take away all the *liabilities*.

ASSET BACKING: See *NAB*, meaning *Net Asset Backing* per share price.

ARBITRAGE: It's when you buy and sell the same or equivalent securities at the same time in different markets to take advantage of a price difference.

ARTICLES OF ASSOCIATION: Paperwork, ahhh paperwork. This red-tape document is mostly for quality assurance, required by company law, to define the rules set down for the internal management of the company. Interesting to share investors occasionally because it shows how the company feels about itself, its goals and guidelines for conduct with customers etc.

ASSOCIATE COMPANY: A company that has between 20% and 50% of its shares owned by another entity.

AT DISCRETION: Your stockbroker calls this the instruction you give them when you tell them to buy/sell shares at the best price they think they can get for you (within a week, usually). You don't have to use the term specifically when you speak to your broker, but if you did, you might say something like: 'Hi, Fred. Can you buy a thousand shares of XYZ for me this week. No rush. At discretion will be fine . . .'

<u>AT LIMIT</u>: The instruction to your stockbroker where you advise the highest price you're prepared to pay or the lowest price you're prepared to sell at. Again, you don't have to mention this techno-jargon. Just tell them your limits.

<u>AT MARKET</u>: The instruction advising your stockbroker that you're prepared to buy or sell at whatever the market price is at the time you give them your order. You won't sound like a jargon nut if you use this one. A typical conversation might go: 'Hi Fred! Can you sell a thousand XYZ for me today please? Yep, at market will be fine.'

BACKDOOR LISTING: If a company fails to meet the stock exchange listing requirements for some reason, they may still achieve listing by purchasing an already listed company and either integrating with it or restructuring new activities into it. This backdoor listing method is sometimes more cost-effective than attempting to meet listing requirements for the primary company.

<u>BEAR</u>: A person who expects prices to fall and sells shares hoping to hibernate for a while and make a profit by buying them again later at a lower price. If they're wrong however, and prices rise instead, then they make a loss instead of a profit. Beginners should not attempt to be bears, unless you've got a safer place to invest your money for a while and/or borrowed money to buy your shares and can't afford to wait out the rise in value again!

BEAR MARKET: A falling market, where a fictitious 'bear' claws down market prices. (Opposite to *bull market*.)

You only make a loss if you sell for less than you buy. If your shares fall in value,

DON'T PANIC!

Consider holding them instead of selling, just as you might for an investment property.

BETA FACTOR: An indicator of an individual stock's volatility, based on how much the price fluctuates on a regular basis. The market is assumed to have a beta of 1, therefore a share price with a beta of 3 would move three times as far in either direction as the rest of the market. Beta factors are therefore used by some professional portfolio managers in limiting the risk levels of the shares in which they choose to invest. Beta factors are not widely available to the general public, however, nor are they really needed in making your final trading decisions (unless you enjoy getting analytical). You can see how volatile a stock is by simply looking up the chart of sale prices for it on the NZSE website at www.nzse.co.nz by clicking on 'listed companies' and choosing the company you're interested in.

BID: How much you're prepared to pay for each share.

<u>BLUE CHIP STOCK</u>: Shares in a company with a good reputation for making profits in good times or bad. Their share price is usually higher than their *net tangible asset value* and although generally more stable in the long term, their *dividend yield* is usually low. Investors who choose to buy blue chip stocks aren't usually interested in making big money fast. They're after slow but reliable progress over the longer term.

BOARD OF DIRECTORS: A group of accountants, business people and occasionally lawyers, ex-sports-men and ex-politicians who are elected by the shareholders to control the planning and imple-mentation of corporate objectives in a company. Directorships may be full- or part-time positions, often enabling directors to be elected to two, three or more company boards at any one time – hopefully gaining experience and business contacts which benefit them all.

BOND: A loan made by you to the government, a semi-government body or a company for a fixed period of time – usually measured in years – at a fixed rate of interest. Similar to an IOU, repayment of the loan and interest is guaranteed by whoever issued the bond, making some – but not all – bonds an arguably safer alternative than shares for timid investors. Exactly how safe depends on who the issuer is; government bonds are considered about as safe as investing gets, but bonds from a small company with loads of debt could be downright risky. As a general guide, the lower the return, the safer a bond is. Just to confuse things, government bonds are also known as 'government stock'. Bonds can be bought and sold through your stockbroker as well as from the issuing body when they are first issued.

BOND MARKET: The combination of places where bonds are bought and sold. As an L-plate investor, you'd buy or sell bonds by phone through your stock-broker who competes for their sale and purchase against other organisations, including professional bond dealers, life assurance companies, banks and other financial institutions.

BONUS ISSUE: As an alternative to paying an increased or bonus dividend, a company may choose to offer 'free' shares to existing shareholders, usually in a predetermined ratio – eg. one bonus share for every three shares held on a certain date, as determined by the company. Sometimes referred to as a *scrip* issue. Share prices often rise afterwards with long-lasting effects on investor confidence.

BOOKS CLOSING DATE: Also known as the record date. The date a company chooses to 'close its books' – like drawing an imaginary line across their financial records – so they can calculate who is entitled to dividends, bonus issues, new issues, etc. at a given time, even if you've only owned their shares for a day. Likewise, it doesn't matter if you've owned their shares for quite a few months beforehand, you will not be entitled to any dividends, bonus issues etc., if you've sold your shares prior to books closing date. See also *ex date* and *cum-dividend*.

BOOM MARKET: A market where prices rise because there are heaps more orders to buy shares (buy orders) than there are people offering to sell (sell offers).

BROKER: A licensed member of the stock exchange who buys and sells stocks, shares and other securities for their clients. However, not all stockbrokers like to deal with small investors, so ask about this when you first ring them seeking to become one of their clients. Stockbrokers come in two varieties these days. There's 'full service' brokers who, as the name suggests, can offer a range of services such as advice and research on specific companies. Then there are 'discount' brokers who don't advise you what to buy or sell, but allow you to trade shares as cheaply as possible, sometimes via the internet.

BROKERAGE: The fee charged by a stockbroker for buying or selling your shares on your behalf. Standard fees for a full service broker are often 2% of the value of the shares bought or sold, with a minimum payment of $40.

Handy hint: Since $40 is also 2% of $2000, it is more cost-effective to keep your buy-and-sell orders above $2000 when dealing with a full service broker. Internet brokerage fees, however, may be as low as $20 because you are often restricted to buying your shares at market and you don't have the benefit of a professional opinion before you make each decision.

BULL: A person who buys shares on the assumption that prices will rise and give them an opportunity to resell later at a profit. Bull calves are L-plate investors who get excited about their opportunities and leap about the market collecting small bundles in various companies hoping to spread their risk, while a stale bull is a disgruntled investor who sells an investment rather than holding onto it in the hope of higher profit later on (sometimes pushing the share price down in the process).

BULL MARKET: A rising market, where an imaginary bull tosses market prices up, or the market charges forward, unpredictably.

CALL: Sometimes companies offer shares that don't require full payment up front. They have a deadline by which to pay the balance in order to make their shares more affordable for the wider population of investors. But it's wise to remember that a 'call' may be made for the payment of part, or all, of the outstanding capital, if the company needs the money unexpectedly before the due date. Holders of shares in *no liability* companies (NL companies) are not liable for the payment (the call) and may forfeit their shares, hence the name no liability. Holders of shares in limited liability companies (LTD Companies) cannot avoid a call and must pay up when asked. You'll know if you're buying shares in either of these kinds of companies, however. The conditions and dates of each part payment for your shares are clearly defined in the prospectus documents and/or on the application form. NOTE: An L-plate investor may come across this kind of offer about once a year.

CALL OPTION: The right to purchase a parcel of shares at a predetermined price within a specific period of time.

CAPITAL GAIN: The profit made by selling some-thing – including shares – for more than you paid for it. Most New Zealand investors assume those profits aren't taxable. That's usually the case, but beware: Inland Revenue *can* treat your share-trading gains as part of your taxable income, if you bought them 'for the purpose of resale' or if it decides you're in the business of share trading. It's a blurry area and most investors won't get caught out, especially if they buy shares with the intention of holding them for the long term. But if you decide to try to make your fortune with a series of quick in-and-out trades, it would pay to speak to your accountant about the tax issue. Unfortunately too many L-plate investors seem to dwell on buying shares mainly for capital gains and overlook the other benefits such as *dividends* and *imputation*. That makes beginners easy prey for big investors who pick up their shares cheaply whenever the market gets the jitters.

CAPITALISATION: In stockmarket terms, this is the value of a company calculated simply as the share price multiplied by the total number of shares on issue by that company. For example, if Kirby's Crusaders & Co (the company run by characters in my children's books) was listed on the stock exchange with a share price of $1.21 with a million shares on issue, then its capitalisation would be 1.21 million. If it had ten million shares on issue at that price, capitalisation would be 12.1 million, and so on.

COMMODITY: Something that's produced, mined or processed to be on-sold for further packaging, manufacturing or development; for example, wool, grain, gold or other primary produce or minerals.

CONTRACT NOTE: The piece of paper sent to a buyer or seller confirming their transaction. It details the purchase/sell price, brokerage payable, stamp duty, GST, and often includes instructions for payment to or from your account. Unlike the FASTER holding statement which graces your letterbox later, your contract note is sent by your broker via post or email as soon as they've 'done your deal'.

CONTRIBUTING SHARES: Shares that are not fully paid, usually in a *no liability* company, but which may be entitled to a *dividend*. See *call*.

CONVERTIBLE NOTE: A fixed interest loan made to a company, much like a *debenture* but with the right to be either redeemed for cash or converted into ordinary shares at a set future date or within a certain period. Just like *shares* and debentures, they can be bought or sold on the stockmarket through your broker.

COUPON: An 'interest voucher' usually associated with bonds and exchangeable for cash on its due date (normally quarterly or half-yearly or yearly).

COVER: Security or cash lodged with a broker under certain circumstances, for example, when the client buys shares without making payment in full.

CUM: An official stockbroking term which means 'with'. For example, a *cum-dividend* means that the shares are being traded so the buyer gets the share with rights to the dividend that's been declared as well. See also *books closing date*.

CUM-DIVIDEND: Described above.

CUM-RIGHTS: Shares quoted 'cum-rights' entitle the buyer to participate in a new or bonus issue of shares that has recently been announced.

Warning!

When buying shares, cum-rights or cum-dividends, beware the share price hasn't risen to consume much of the value of the temporary bonuses, because share prices may just as easily fall after books closing date or rights-offer deadlines.

CUMULATIVE: Some *preference shares* have a right to receive a dividend for each financial period even though no dividend has been declared. If it doesn't get paid then it goes into arrears for possible payment later when the company can better afford to pay out.

DAISY CHAIN: An illegal market-rigging scam where a group of traders actively buys *securities* in a particular company to give the impression of a healthy demand for it. But then as soon as the genuine unsuspecting investors have been drawn in, the bad guys sell to cash in profits leaving the poor suckers with no genuine buyers left in the collapsed market.

DAY TRADING (DAYLIGHT TRADING, JOBBING THE MARKET): When you buy and sell out of the market within the same day or trading session in order to avoid holding an 'overnight position'.

DEAD CAT BOUNCE: A false or phantom recovery, usually when economic activity in a company has fallen so low that it must turn up when a good dividend or increased profit is announced. But if the big investors remain unimpressed and unconvinced of the prospects for a meaningful recovery, or if they're distracted by more impressive opportunities elsewhere then the price may plummet again.

DEBENTURE: A fixed interest loan you make to a company for a fixed period, secured by company assets, therefore the level of safety/security depends on the financial strength of the company concerned. Like shares and bonds, debentures can also be bought or sold through your stockbroker, or directly from organisations such as finance companies.

DEBT FUNDING: Borrowing money for use by a company by way of debentures, loans or increasing other liabilities. Debt funding is an alternative to *equity funding*.

DELISTED: When a company's shares are no longer allowed to be traded on the stock exchange.

DEPRECIATION: Amounts charged to financial records to provide for that part of the cost or book value of a fixed asset which is not recoverable – usually because of age – when it is finally put out of use. *Handy hint:* Depreciation schedules are listed in company annual reports. Beware of companies who make these columns of figures difficult for beginners to read or understand.

DIRECTORS: See *board of directors*.

DISCOUNT: The amount that a security is quoted below its face value. (Opposite to *premium*.) Sounds complicated in many financial reports, but it works much the same way as discounts at Woolworths. Eg. if a share is worth $2 and is for sale at the moment for $1.80, you're getting it for a 10% discount of 20 cents.

DIVIDEND: A payment which is usually made twice a year to distribute part of a company's net profit to shareholders as a reward for investing in the company. The dividend paid near the middle of the financial year is called an interim dividend, while the dividend paid near the end of the financial year is called the final dividend. All dividends are usually expressed as cents per share, and may or may not have *imputation credits* which can be used to reduce your tax bill.

Handy hints

To maximise your minimum returns from shares without having to worry about buying or selling regularly, simply buy shares in reputable companies which have a long history of paying fully *imputed dividends* even during depressed economies. (Your broker can supply a list.) This way, you'll not only get the dividend paid to you at least twice a year, you'll also have the tax paid on this income at the company tax rate by the company. In this way, you'll have much less tax to pay and may even get a refund, depending on your tax bracket.

For tax bracket details see Chapter 6 of *Your Investment Property*, or the 'Before we begin' section of *Your Mortgage*.

DIVIDEND RATE: Dividend per share in dollars × 100 to convert to cents, then divided by the *par value*, but not as easy to use by beginners as the *dividend yield*, which is also more freely available to the general public. Unless you pay heaps for a software program to watch share prices and calculate the dividend rate for you, you'll have to calculate it by hand. Easy to do, but time-consuming, so I never worry. By comparison, the dividend yield is published regularly wherever share prices are quoted, and is one of the top five things I look for when buying shares. (*EPS*, *NTA*, *P/E ratio* and share price being the others.)

DIVIDEND REINVESTMENT PLAN (DRP):

Some companies offer you the choice of having your dividend paid to you in shares credited to your portfolio instead of cash deposited to your bank account. This gives investors the chance to get extra shares in the company without having to pay a stockbroking fee. Some companies even offer you the DRP shares a few percent cheaper than you could buy them through the stockmarket. But you have to keep good records for your tax and tell your stockbroker that you're participating in the DRP at the time you decide to sell, or else you could end up with a small *unmarketable parcel*.

DIVIDEND YIELD: Dividend per share in dollars ×
100 to convert to cents, then divided by the last known share price. The dividend yield is very useful to L-plate investors when deciding which stocks to buy, since it's the dividend shown as a percentage of

the last sale price and is published daily in major newspapers such as the *New Zealand Herald* or the *Dominion-Post,* among other places. You must remember, however, that this is a historical figure. The next dividend to be declared may be higher or lower than the last one, depending on profits. Also, since the div' yield is calculated daily based on current prices, your actual yield may be higher or lower depending on how much you paid for the shares at another date.

Example: You buy 1000 shares at $2 each and your neighbour buys their 1000 shares of the same company at $2.50 either before or after you. Then if the company pays a half-yearly 16 cent dividend, you will both get paid $160 (1000 × $0.16) but *your* dividend will be a dividend yield of 8% ($160 × 100 ÷ $2000) for the six-month period, whereas your neighbour's yield will only be 6.4% for the same period ($160 × 100 ÷ $2500), because he spent more money buying his shares. At the same time, yields may be reported to be as low as 2% in market reports if the current share price has risen to $8 each. NOTE: Unlike a term deposit, the length of time you both own the shares has nothing to do with it (ex-dates and books closing dates notwithstanding).

Did you know?

Stocks with no yields are the ones that don't pay dividends at all. Their directors are either expecting investors will benefit from a fast rise in the share price eventually/soon. Or they're re-investing every cent they can into the business to either survive hardship, maximise competitiveness or fund expansion (hopefully without over-compensating their own pockets in the process). Resource stocks are the most likely companies to withhold dividends, however blue chips and other industrial stocks have been known to withhold yields until hardships are overcome from time to time too.

Stocks with low yields are either barely coping with their regular returns to investors, or they expect investors to be happy with their slow but steady growth in the share price. Dog stocks and blue chips are therefore the most likely companies to offer regularly low yields – unhappy bedfellows in this category, however, which is why you must always look beyond computer reports and market reports into logical analysis of what the company is up to, before choosing which companies to buy shares in.

Stocks with high yields are often ranked low by a rating agency when the high returns are offered as an enticement for investors which may otherwise pass them over. Chances for regular capital growth may be either lower or erratic for a number of reasons, however. (For example, a large reliable company operating in a mature industry which is no longer growing or is tightly competitive. Or perhaps a lively young company may be highly profitable during certain seasons but hasn't yet proven its reliability over consecutive years.)

Handy hint: Investments in high yield companies are generally the most likely to give investors the highest returns in both yield and capital growth (often 20% to 80% per year), provided that shares are purchased during the down-cycle, resold on the rise again after a dividend payment and re-purchased on the down-cycle again ready for the next rise. The risk, of course, is that the next down-cycle will last longer than expected, rises may not be as high as the last time, or the company may go bust during a down-cycle and sudden change in competitors or economy – one reason why you should always keep a close eye on the *EPS* and *NTA* when purchasing such stocks.

Beware of companies that appear in market reports as high yielding because of a once-off large dividend to investors, because those dividends may not be repeated, yet may have lifted the share price to insupportable levels. Also beware of companies that would normally offer a low yield, but whose share price, EPS and perhaps also NTA has dropped sharply since the last dividend making it much harder for them to pay the next dividend at all, let alone at the same level as last time.

DOG STOCKS: Investments that bite the hands that buy them and often give you a good chomp in the backside as well. These are companies which pay slack or no dividends, have a share price that doesn't understand the words 'up, boy, up!', and which report major losses while their directors are busy choosing the colour of their next Porsche.

DOW JONES INDEX: A New York measure of stock-market performance using the average closing prices from 30 American stocks. These stocks are drawn from mature industries such as chemicals and steel, while modern high-tech stocks are generally overlooked. Interestingly, the index is named after Charles Dow and Eddie Jones who in 1882 began reporting stock-market news from their small Wall Street office to New York's financial community, which subsequently inspired the birth of the *Wall Street Journal* with Charles Dow taking on the role of first editor.

EARNINGS PER SHARE (EPS): The company's net profit divided by the total number of shares in the company and expressed as cents per share. It's another good indicator for investors choosing which shares to buy or sell.

Handy hint

If the EPS is negative then the company is recording losses, not profits. Rarely a good reason to buy, unless the company has announced a major financial or product overhaul. See also *P/E ratios*.

On the other hand, a high EPS (say 30% or more of the share price) is a good thing. If companies are making good profits, their share price can't stay low for long.

ENTITLEMENTS ISSUE: Another method for companies to raise capital working funds other than through ordinary shares. Entitlements issues are more common to no liability companies where existing shareholders can buy new shares in the company at a discount to the current market price. Shares are usually allotted in a ratio of one new share for every 'so many' shares held. Unlike a rights issue, an entitlement issue is not transferable, and therefore cannot be sold. ie. it is *non-renounceable*.

ETHICAL INVESTMENTS: Also called green, socially responsible or conscience investments. Not to be confused with *green chip shares*, these companies or managed trusts are dedicated to achieving sustainable environments and societies. Sceptics might lump these with the dog stocks, because of risk of non-profitability, particularly in the short term. This approach to investing is relatively new in New Zealand.

<u>EQUITY</u>: Ownership of something that has a reasonable resale value. If it's ownership in a company, then it's usually through ordinary shares. (Debentures and *unsecured notes* are debt rather than equity.) If you borrowed money to buy the investment, then equity = the asset's current value minus the debt owing on the loan.

EQUITY FUNDING: The issuing of new shares at *par* or at a *premium*. It's an alternative to debt-funding.

EX: The opposite to 'cum' and means 'without'. An *ex-dividend* means the shares are being traded without the current dividend, so the seller gets to keep the declared dividend instead of the buyer getting it. Shares traded without the current bonus, right or entitlement issues are also quoted 'ex'.

EXCHANGE TRADED OPTIONS: These *put* or call options can be dynamic and potentially powerful investment tools because of their hedging and trading opportunities, but they are not a good place for beginners to wet their investment feet, because of increased risk in trading and the time and dedication needed to stay on top of them.

EX-DATE: This is the date on which shares change from being quoted 'cum' to 'ex'. It's the next business day after the record date (also known as the books closing date).

EX-DIVIDEND: Once shares are quoted ex-dividend, it means the buyer is not entitled to the recently announced dividend. New Zealand shares typically go ex-dividend on a Monday. *Handy hint:* Beware that the share price will often fall by the amount of the dividend (approx.) once a share goes ex-dividend.

EX-RIGHTS: Shares and other securities that are quoted 'ex-rights' entitle the seller to retain the right to participate in a recently declared new issue.

FACE VALUE: See *par*.

FASTER: This stands for Fully Automated Screen Trading and Electronic Registration System and it's the system that stock exchange members use to trade shares. It's a computerised marketplace, which has replaced the old stock exchange trading floor where brokers used to shout out their buy and sell orders.

Did you know?

Before **FASTER**, companies had to issue printed share certificates for each new buyer as proof of ownership. Delays in settlement were therefore long and risk of lost certificates was high. But since the introduction of the new computerised system, where share certificates have been replaced by electronic records with holding statements issued whenever changes occur, settlement of sales and purchases can now be finalised within 3 days. (See *T+3*.) Lost certificates are no longer a worry either.

FASTER automatically records share deals, so sellers can receive payment in a few days. As a bonus, any processing errors during purchase or sale of securities have the benefit of insurance guarantees from funds set aside under the FASTER system. See also *T+3*.

FIN: Faster Identification Number. For share investors, it's the equivalent of the PIN number you use at your bank. When you first buy shares, you'll be allocated a FIN number which you'll have to quote if you want to sell shares in future. The FIN counts as proof of ownership, so keep it safe. Because there are several share registries, you may end up with several FIN numbers, although the stock exchange is working to make sure that each investor has just one FIN.

FINAL DIVIDEND: See *dividend*.

FIXED INTEREST: A security where the return (when held to maturity) is fixed, but periodic interest payments are usually made with principal paid at maturity. *Handy hint:* Beware of heavy exit penalties in the fine print before signing into a fixed interest agreement in case you need to withdraw your money from the scheme early.

FLOAT: When a company first sells shares to the public. A company 'floats' on the stockmarket only after it has fulfilled all NZSE-listing rules – which are often stricter than those required under company law – in order for it to allow members of the public to buy shares and other securities in it. *Handy hint:* Buying shares through a float has the extra benefit of being free of brokerage and stamp duty costs, even if you submit application forms through your broker, because the *underwriter* has organised to cover these costs already from the company.

FUTURES: A futures contract is an agreement to buy or sell a set quantity of a commodity, (including foreign currency or bank bills of exchange) on a set future date and at an agreed price, depending on when the contract is traded on the futures exchange. It's a binding contract enforceable by law, but where trading used to be conducted via frantic screaming from the trading room floor of the Futures Exchange, such stressful 'outcrying' has thankfully been phased out by the introduction of computer screen trading.

GILT-EDGED: These are securities that have a reputation for stability, usually government or semi-government stocks.

GREEN CHIP SHARES: Shares in a growing company which has begun to make good profits and is returning high dividend yields to shareholders. Green chip shares are usually priced lower than blue chip shares and can be either cyclical or experience greater annual price fluctuations. See also *industrial leaders* and *resource leaders*.

To help remember the difference between blue and green chip shares, try thinking that:

Blue chip shares are blue like the sky: they have cloudy grey days too, but are usually same old reliable blue sky, same old dividend, with capital growth much like the hole in the ozone layer: growing bigger, but slowly.

Green chip shares are green like trees: They start small, have cyclical seasons of growth, bear the sweetest fruit in good times, die back a little in harsh times, and while some may die completely in sudden climate changes, most will thrive with proper long-term management and care.

GROWTH STOCK: Stock with potential for expansion (and therefore capital gain too). However, immediate income prospects from dividends aren't likely to be generous because the company is using every spare cent to fund expansion or development.

HANG SENG: The Hang Seng Index is Hong Kong's equivalent of the NZSE-50, the US Dow Jones, Australia's All Ordinaries and Japan's Nikkei.

HEDGE FUND: Lingo for a very strictly managed private portfolio of cash and/or leveraged funds, usually limited to big investors who attempt to make low-risk profits using every investment tool known to man and pooling funds to attract the biggest brains in the business to manage it. Performance incentives (a generous share in the capital growth) are often paid to managers in addition to their management fees, however hedge fund managers – sometimes called a 'general partner' – often invest their own money as well to help guarantee dedication and performance. Much like a plane crash, therefore, the only time L-plate investors usually hear about them is when something goes wrong. Each fund relies on the specialist expertise of the manager, who often sticks to their tightly focused investment strategy, for example, short selling or playing equities with both long and short positions. So each fund is only as good as the pilot in control. (See also *long position*, *short position*.)

HOLDING COMPANY: A company which owns the controlling number of shares in one or more other companies, usually in order to control the finance, management and marketing of the 'held' company and its subsidiaries, rather than for investment purposes.

HOSTILE TAKEOVER: See *takeover*.

HOT MONEY: Investment funds which jump in and out of investments, sometimes staying only overnight while in search of the 'hottest' returns.

HURT MONEY: The deposit or funds deposited into an offset account in order to get a loan for investment, or to keep your margin lending account provider happy in the event of a call. In the case of a *margin lending* account for example, if the value of the shares fall, your margin lender will make a demand for more 'hurt' money.

HYBRID SECURITIES: Some companies occasionally offer more complicated methods of investing in them which may be either more or less extensive than their ordinary shares. Returns are usually higher than for the ordinary shares, however unit costs and risk may be proportionately higher too. Also, hybrid securities can be for limited periods and dividends may or may not be fully imputed, despite predictions. These hybrid securities may include *convertible notes*, an investment which offers a set interest rate for a set term, and can then convert into ordinary shares at a specified date.

IMPUTATION (IMPUTATION CREDIT): In the bad old days, dividends paid by companies (out of their after-tax income) were taxed all over again when investors received them. Since 1 April 1988 the company tax can be distributed (imputed) to shareholders when they get their dividend through imputation credits. Shareholders can then claim those imputation credits in their annual tax returns to reduce the tax payable on their income. Imputation credits therefore have the effect of making the dividend yield better than the equivalent yield on savings accounts and term deposits after tax. Eg. If a term deposit at a bank pays 5% interest and a fully imputed dividend also pays a 5% return, then the dividend will leave you better off after tax, because you still have to pay tax on the term deposit interest. But the fully imputed dividend is paid to you AFTER 33% company tax is sent to Inland Revenue. So if you're in the 21% tax bracket, then your 33% imputation credit will mean you've overpaid tax on your dividend by 12% and can claim it back. Imputation can be a godsend for investors, but remember that not all companies pay fully imputed dividends – it depends how much company tax they pay. *Handy hint:* Check for an 'I' code before investing if you want to take advantage of full imputation credits.

IMPUTED DIVIDEND: A dividend which is entitled to an *imputation credit*, for claiming against your personal tax based on the tax which the company has already paid to Inland Revenue. The level of imputation for fully imputed shares is assumed to be 33% (the current company tax rate) unless otherwise stated. Shares can be partially imputed, however. In some market reports the level of imputation is indicated by a code letter, such as 'I' for a fully imputed dividend and 'P' for one which is partially imputed. Other reports show the actual amount of the imputation credit, in cents. If there are no imputation credits it means that no tax has been paid on the dividend, therefore just like interest on a term deposit, you may have to pay tax on it at the end of the year. See also *dividend* and *imputation credits*.

INSIDE INFORMATION: Confidential information available to a small number of people that would affect the share price of a company if made public. Profiteering from inside information, either by selling the information or through share trading, is illegal. Regulations are in place to ensure that all investors get equal access to information which may affect the share price of a company from day to day. However, employees can still learn of probable upcoming contracts long before signatures are on paper and the market is advised, so do be very careful of making share purchase decisions in your own name where you may be accused of profiteering from decisions which haven't yet been made public.

> Never do business with close friends or relatives, unless there's absolutely no way on earth for you to get angry, accused of insider trading or disappointed over conditions during purchases, management or sales.
>
> In other words, never. Business partners may come and go, but busted relationships have a way of haunting your budget forever.

INSTITUTION: An entity with large investable funds, eg. pension or superannuation funds, insurance and assurance companies and money lenders.

INTERIM DIVIDEND: A dividend paid during the financial year instead of at the end. Most profitable companies pay dividends every half-year.

JOBBING THE MARKET: See *day trading*.

JOINT VENTURE: An agreement between two or more parties who agree to jointly explore, finance or participate in a particular project or development.

KILLER BEE: An individual, investment bank or other firm employed by one company to help beat a hostile *takeover* bid.

LEVERAGE: This refers to the process of increasing the amount of money you have available to invest, by borrowing money from somewhere else.

LIABILITIES: These are items or money owed by a person or company to another person or company. Store accounts, professional IOUs and the unpaid portions of loans are all liabilities which can tip the balance between approval or disapproval of your next investment loan if the bank isn't happy with your balance of assets, liabilities, current income and potential to earn more.

LIMITED LIABILITY (LTD): The liability of the shareholder in this type of company is limited to how much you still owe on your shares. See also *call*.

LISTED STOCK: Securities in companies which are approved to be traded to the general public on the stock exchange. Telecom, Carter Holt Harvey and Air New Zealand, for instance, are all listed companies, while your local mechanic, plumber or doctor are probably all unlisted companies.

LIQUIDATOR: A person or company appointed – either by a special resolution of shareholders or by a court order – to take charge of another person or company that is unable to repay their debts and is therefore declared bankrupt, 'wound up' and closed down – or in rare cases, sold off to a third party who can restore profitability. The liquidator is supposed to ensure that all people and companies who are owed money by the bankrupt entity are repaid as much as possible of what is owed to them. Sadly, however, liquidators often take so long to bring matters to a close, and charge such exorbitant fees, that their costs eat giant holes in the money left over to distribute to the people and companies who were owed the money in the first place. See also *winding up*.

LONG POSITION: Actually owning the securities you're about to sell or with minimum debt. It's the opposite of being 'short'. See also *short position*.

MARGIN: Money or stocks put up by a client to a stockbroker in part payment for the purchase of stock under a forward contract – much like the deposit you'd put down on a property, but these contracts can be a lot more complicated. If the value of your investment property falls, for example, you're not expected to pay a lump sum to make sure you don't owe more than 80% of a property's market value, but with margin lending for stockmarket *securities*, you may have to, or else be forced to sell your shares.

MARGIN CALL: See *margin lending* below.

MARGIN LENDING: Not something I'd ever use as an L-plate investor, although some loan providers would have us think they're the in-thing (or sometimes, the only thing) suitable for financing our stockmarket investments. Advantages are that we may get lower interest rates and great discounts on brokerage fees for doing all our trading business through our lender. Access to regular market reports and ease of payment procedures may also be provided. However, these revolving credit-style accounts often place limitations on which companies we're permitted to invest in. Of

---

Warning

If your shares drop in value to a point where your loan is now 70% or more of the value of the asset, there is often a 5% margin before your lender will 'call' for more hurt money or shares to be signed over to it, but because their aim is to keep under 80%, calls may be made closer to 70% if the market is dropping quickly.

greater concern may be that we're rarely permitted to owe more than 70% or 80% of the asset's current market value – which means that if the value of some or all of the shares fall, we'll get a margin call, where we must either sell the shares at their reduced value, or pay a lump sum immediately, much like an extra deposit on a property when the mortgage insurers refuse your initial loan application. But in this case, a margin call can be issued at any time and for as many times necessary during the life of the loan, so our maximum debt is never more than 80% of the asset's current value. Having a margin lending account often subjects you to their regular newsletters too, which often encourage investors to maximise debt, undermine safety-nets and place investment portfolios at greatest risk and higher maintenance costs, all in the interests of chasing potentially greater profits. The greatest disadvantage of these accounts can therefore be that your lender is in the perfect position to purchase your shares for a song whenever you're placed in a position where you have to sell. And since you may do all your trading through them too, a disreputable broker may even time your sale and their re-purchase to best maximise your loss and their profits – and you'd never know. See also *hurt money*.

Handy hints

- If you wish to borrow to start your shares portfolio, then start small. I use a large unsecured overdraft with a credit union, which has a small (optional extra) insurance fee so that if I die, my debt is 'forgiven' making all of my purchases on that account debt free. The account swings from being heavily overdrawn to heavily in credit throughout the month, depending on when I need higher cash reserves on hand, so I made sure this account is one that also pays high interest whenever I'm in credit. (NOTE: It looks weird on a monthly statement, but it's quite common to have two entries for interest. One entry is credited to pay me for interest on the days my excess funds put my account into 'the black'. The other is for interest charged for the days my overdraft had a negative balance.)

- Of course all interest and fees related to your investment purchase are always tax deductible, no matter which kind of loan you use, provided that clear accounting records are kept. So I choose loans which don't require me to tell my lender when I'm withdrawing money from the account or why. I also make sure my lender can't try to regulate which kinds of shares I should buy or sell – or when.

- An alternative method for funding your loan purchases – particularly suited to cash buyers, irregular investors or investors who are positively gearing – may therefore be to operate a separate mortgage offset account, which consists of 'equity' borrowed from the property to opportunity-buy shares whenever other cash reserves are a little low. But ownership of my own home first would always remain my first priority.

- While you're learning the sharemarket, you should never invest funds unless you can live without them. It's true that you can sell shares and get paid for them within three days (see **T+3**), but ideally, to maximise your profits, you need to give them time to grow and pay dividends, so you need to be able to lock them up for six to twelve months at a time – or longer – just as you would for any good term deposit account. Therefore do NOT invest your bill savings or grocery money on the sharemarket, unless you get your kicks out of risk, loss and misery.

MARKET CRASH/SLUMP: Most investors and *quasi investors* pack death at the sound of this. To think their shares could be losing value on a daily basis indefinitely is the stuff of their nightmares. However, for the small investor, cash buyers and some investors who positively gear, it's a time of increased opportunity, a chance to profit from those investors who got in too deep, misjudged the market, or couldn't afford to hold onto their shares until prices rose again because of repayment pressure from their debts or their own fears. Investors who use margin lending accounts to borrow money for share purchases are also at greater risk of having to sell during market slumps, because their lenders may 'call' in their debts when values drop to a point where they no longer have the required equity (usually 20%). They'll have to either cough up a lump sum from somewhere else or sell shares to those investors who can afford to buy in at that price and wait.

MARKET PRICE: The current prevailing price to buy or sell a security on the open market.

MARKET REPORTS: These come in three forms:
1) Tables of statistics which are reliably published in many newspapers the next day, or free within 20 minutes on the internet through the NZSE website at www.nzse.co.nz. NOTE: Some stockbrokers and various share-trading software

packages may offer live feed prices, but usually as part of their much higher costs. Your own stockbroker, however, will usually tell you the live prices over the phone for free at any time you may wish to discuss a particular purchase or sale.

2) TV, mobile phone and radio market reports are usually accurate to within 24 hours.

3) Printed stories in newspapers, magazines and periodicals about industry and company performances should be considered as a guide only unless specific dates are quoted because articles may be published a week to four months after the journalist wrote the article (due to publishing deadlines) and the time it takes to edit, print and distribute the reports.

MEMORANDUM OF ASSOCIATION: This is the initial legal document in the incorporation of a company which states full details of the company, its powers and objectives.

MINIMUM HOLDING: The smallest number of a particular share that you can own. How big that number is depends on the price of the share in question – if they're worth $10-plus you can own just 25 shares, but if the price is 25c or less you'll have to own at least 2000. Beware of dealing in small numbers of shares – even the minimum *brokerage* charge will be expensive in relation to the value of the shares.

MONEY MARKET: A general term referring to the trading of treasury notes, money and other short-term securities by banks and other financial institutions.

MOODY'S: Moody's Investors Service is a US-based corporate credit rating agency, founded in 1903 by John Moody, but merged with Dun and Bradstreet in 1961. Best known internationally for its global credit rating research and risk analysis (on government and commercial entities in over 100 countries).

MORTGAGE: Security taken over a property to provide a large loan.

NASDAQ: Pronounced Naz-dak, the term was coined in America as an acronym for National Association of Securities Dealers Automated Quotations, which means the process of ordering buy-and-sell contracts over the phone and by computer. It was born informally when brokers and investors started calling each other by phone to discuss orders, but was formalised on computer in the early 1970s and has since become its own word. Like the NZSE, the Nasdaq doesn't have a physical trading floor and there are no market specialists to buy any unfilled orders.

NET ASSET BACKING (NAB, also known as ASSET BACKING or NET ASSET VALUE): An important check for investors! Net asset backing is

where net assets of a company in dollars are divided by the total number of shares issued. Eg. If Thingy Inc has $100,000 in net assets and 10,000 shares issued, then it has a net asset backing of $10.00 per share. Then compare this to the company's earning capacity (see **EPS**) and share price to see if you're onto a good deal.

NET TANGIBLE ASSET BACKING (NTA):

Slightly different to NAB, it's the net assets owned by shareholders of a company at balance date – and is the net asset value per share. Technically speaking for a moment, it's the total shareholders' funds, less intangibles, less preference capital, divided by the number of ordinary shares. Basically, this is the underlying value of the naked share, after funds are set aside to pay off debts, assuming things do go bad. *Handy hint:* If your local paper reports a column for the NTAs instead of the NABs, don't panic. The NTAs are just as useful, if not more so, when making comparisons alongside the company's EPS and share price and when short-listing which companies you're ready to buy or sell.

NEW SHARES: Recently issued shares are called 'new shares' when they don't yet rank equally with existing shares in their entitlement to dividends.

NIKKEI: Officially called the Nikkei 225 Index, it's Japan's equivalent to our NZSE-50 index and as the name suggests, is calculated using final sale prices each day from the top 225 companies listed on the Tokyo stock exchange.

NO LIABILITY: New Zealand laws allow mining companies to register as a 'no liability' company. This means that shareholders cannot be sued for payment of any call made on part-paid shares, but if they fail to pay a call, their shares are forfeited.

NON-RENOUNCEABLE RIGHTS: These rights (or entitlements) are unable to be sold on the open market. See also *rights.*

NOMINAL CAPITAL (also known as REGISTERED or AUTHORISED CAPITAL): This is the total dollar value of shares that the company is registered as having, as stated in their Memorandum of Association or authorised by subsequent resolution of shareholders.

NZSE: <u>**NEW ZEALAND STOCK EXCHANGE**</u>. See their website at www.nzse.co.nz for free access to sales data, research, media alerts and performance charts for each company listed on the stock exchange. The NZSE also issues each company with a unique three-letter code which can be found by looking under 'listed companies' on its website. *Handy hint:* Have a list of the codes for the companies you wish to research at your side each time you log on to the net and you'll be able to navigate their website much faster.

<u>NZSE-50 INDEX</u>: This cranky little statistic can be temperamental at best. It's a tease really, because it's calculated on the share prices of 50 NZSE-listed companies, but you'll rarely own shares in more than 20 companies. The NZSE-50 should really be used by beginners as a guide only – just an overview of how the market in general traded on any given day. Remember that a major dive in share price of a big blue chip company – for example Telecom, which can account for more than 30 percent of the NZSE-50 – can plummet the index, when in fact all other companies are doing just fine. So if you don't invest in any of those 50 companies at all, the NZSE-50 is – from a practical point of view – not applicable to you.

You'll never get rich by following the pack.

ODD LOT: A small parcel of shares which is considered less than marketable. See also *marketable parcel*.

OFFER: See *ask*.

OFFICIAL LIST: The list of securities that are allowed to be traded on the stock exchange.

OPERATOR: An employee of a broking company who performs some of the duties of a stockbroker, but who is not actually licensed as a stockbroker with the NZSE. NZSE rules say that anyone who works for a firm which is a member of the exchange and who advises the public must be at least an associate member of the exchange.

OPTION: This is your right to take up certain stock on specified terms by a specified time. Options are usually transferable and can be bought and sold. See also *call option* and *exchange traded options*.

ORDER: Your instructions to your stockbroker to buy or sell shares or other securities.

PAR: The nominal or stated value given to shares in the Articles of Association of a company, but has no relation to the asset value or actual worth of the shares. It's used to give calculations and forecasts an underlying stability, but it's not something I've ever flustered my knickers over when choosing which companies' shares to buy or sell.

PARTLY PAID SHARES: See *contributing shares*.

PLACEMENT: An allotment of shares, debentures or other types of *securities* made directly from the company to selected investors.

PORTFOLIO: All your investments can be included in your portfolio, which is basically a stamp-album of

your assets. Your house, cash, savings accounts, investment properties, valuable jewellery, shares etc., can all
be considered part of your portfolio. Some people
even consider their health or ability to learn new
things as intangible assets within their portfolio. Wise
investors aim for a mixed portfolio which doesn't put
all their 'financial eggs' into just one or two baskets,
and a stockbroker can help you plan your portfolio
(not always for a fee) or double-check the portfolio
that you put together by following this book.

Beware of the investment advisor who earns an
annual percentage, lump sum payment or sly
kickback from your investments AND tries to get
you to buy into those investments when either:

a) you must contribute to the fund for years before you
   start to see major benefits, or . . .

b) if your common sense or instincts are screaming
   for you to back away.

PREFERENCE SHARES: These shares usually have
a fixed and often higher dividend rate than ordinary
shares, but are also much more expensive to buy.
They rank above ordinary shares when it comes to
bankruptcy claims on assets, earnings and dividends,

but they rank below creditors and debenture holders, by which time the liquidators have usually made sure their fees have eaten away their worth anyhow. It's always best to get out of a share when the indicators tell you to (not necessarily if market reports are scaring you). If you wait until the massive loss announcements hit the headlines, it's often too late, no matter which kind of share you own.

PREMIUM: This is the amount by which a security is quoted or issued above its par value, and is the opposite to *discount*. If the shares are for sale for a large premium, it means the existing shareholders or other investors in general are expecting you to compensate them for selling their shares now, before the price rises even further.

PRICE/EARNINGS RATIO (P/E RATIO, PE RATIO): The market price of a share, divided by the company's earnings per share. Translated roughly, this means 'the number of times you are paying for their current earnings'. As a general rule, the P/E ratio is a handy indicator for beginners because it tells you how the big investors 'really' expect a company to perform. If you compare companies operating in similar fields, then a low P/E ratio indicates that most sharemarket traders think that one company will have a poorer performance than its competitors with

---

Handy hint

When buying shares at a premium, be sure you're not being sucked in by market hype, which more often than not is fuelled by large investors simply trying to offload their shares to less experienced buyers at a good price before the market falls. In other words, market hype is often a crock of slightly stale horse manure. There are many other reasons, however, so if you can't find the premium details published with your stock reports, then check out the company's website, call your broker, or look up their last annual report. It's often listed in the table of vital statistics near the front, but don't sweat too much if you can't find it. There are far more important indicators that can help you.

---

higher P/E ratios. A high P/E ratio, however, can mean either that the company is expected to do well, or that it is being valued on a good asset backing. A dash in the P/E column is nothing to worry about, however. Many companies have delays in reporting. If your broker can't advise on the company's current status, or if you can't find all the info you need on a company, just buy something else. Bargains are everywhere.

Handy hint

When starting my own shares portfolio or whenever I'm a bit suspicious of the market, I look for companies with a P/E ratio between 6 and 14. You can still make good profits buying shares with P/E ratios outside this bracket, but it's usually a little riskier. P/Es over 20 however are often considered overpriced. Whereas shares with a negative EPS and P/E between 6 and 14 could be interesting investments to watch. Shares with a low P/E and a negative EPS, may still be a good investment for capital growth if it's a reputable company with an unusual reason for their temporary losses, but you may have to wait a year or more to see growth and profits return. That's when you'll double or treble your money.

PROSPECTUS: This is the initial document – usually a sizeable booklet – that is issued free of charge by a company to potential investors, and which sets out the terms of its equity issue or debt raising. It is subject to company law and the stringent rules of the stock exchange. Although technically open to the public, sometimes only regular clients of stockbrokers who have been selected by the company can get hold of a 'hot' or limited issue prospectus. There are no stockbroking fees on shares that you buy using the application form from the back of a prospectus, even if you fill it in and post it back to your stockbroker for processing.

> Be suspicious of a 'glossy' prospectus with lots of big pictures and small print.

PROXY: If you can't make it to a special or annual general meeting of a company in which you are a shareholder, then you can give written authorisation for someone else (a friend, workmate or perhaps even the chairman of the meeting) to be your proxy; that is, to be your stunt-double who votes on your behalf at the company meeting. Beware: SOME motions (suggestions for a decision to be made) are voted on by only those shareholders who actually managed to turn up. A show of hands is sometimes requested from those present, regardless of whether you've cast your vote by proxy or not. (Another reason to beware of companies who hold their annual general meetings or special meetings close to public holidays or national days of celebration when minor shareholders would much rather be at the beach.)

PUT OPTIONS: An Option contract that entitles the taker to sell a fixed number of shares of the underlying security at a stated price on or before a fixed expiry date. Not a trick for beginners or investors who prefer to avoid enslavement to their stock reports. You need to be right on the ball with your calendar, knowledge of the company, the market and then judge when is the best time to get out or wait until expiry.

QUASI INVESTORS: The ones who talk about the sharemarket as if they're old timers, but who never actually buy anything, OR investors who don't own any shares other than those which were 'given' to them when their insurance companies etc. listed on the NZSE. Sadly, quasi investors are very often our mums and dads or grandparents, who are usually at the greatest risk of becoming targets of investment scams through their inexperience and isolation from market information. If you do know anyone in this bracket, I therefore encourage you to share your copy of this book with them, as they would not normally purchase it for themselves, but may be the ones who need it the most.

RALLY: A short, energetic price rise in either the market generally or in a particular company's share price. Often a good time to sell. Rarely a good time to buy, unless it's a good company selling a good product AND the *P/E ratios* and other indicators mentioned in this book are within their recommended levels.

REACTION: A temporary price weakness that sometimes comes after a sharp upswing or rally. If a news reporter says the market 'reacted today' they're supposed to mean the market fell; however, I have heard the term used in the non-jargon sense, meaning that the market reacted either up or down to a specific event. Confusing sometimes, so best to keep your thoughts non-committal on this one, I think.

RECESSION: When the economy slows down quickly and gross national or domestic product (income from intra-New Zealand sales and/or international sales) falls in two consecutive quarters. Often accompanied by rising unemployment and falling interest rates, there is often a fine line between recession and depression.

RECONSTRUCTION: Also known as consolidation. Sometimes, a company might have to adjust its capital issues by reconstructing its shares into units of greater face value. Eg. A share may shoot from $2 to $6 each, but where you had say, 3000 shares beforehand, you may have only 1000 shares afterwards. It's opposite to *share splitting*, by the way, both of which often result in a short but rapid rise in value afterwards, if it's done effectively by proficient managers.

RENOUNCEABLE RIGHTS: These are rights (entitlements or promises of goodwill, such as promised dividends or upcoming shareholder discounts) that can be bought and sold as part of the share price on the open market. See also *rights*.

RESERVE BANK OF NEW ZEALAND: New Zealand's head-honcho bank, created in 1934. The bank is in the public eye whenever its boss, known as the Governor, goes public (usually once every three months) and announces whether interest rates will rise or fall by some fraction of a percent, or stay the same. Under the Reserve Bank Act of 1989, the bank has the job of 'maintaining price stability', ie keeping inflation under control. The bank's other jobs include issuing new notes and coins, supervising the banking system and registering new banks. It also acts as the 'banks' banker' by providing accounts which banks can use to make payments to each other. And when the Government wants to borrow some money, the Reserve Bank raises the funds by selling *bonds* and *Treasury bills*.

RIGHTS: A privilege granted to shareholders to buy new shares in the same company, usually below the prevailing market price. A right can either be exercised or sold and is usually issued in a predetermined ratio; for example, one right for every four shares held. See also *renounceable rights* and *non-renounceable rights*.

SCRIP: This is a document with an identifying number which states that you're a registered holder of a number of shares or other securities. The most common form of scrip is a share certificate, but electronic trading and FASTER certificates are making these obsolete.

Handy hint

One good indication that the sharemarket is about to rise is a drop in interest rates followed a few days or weeks later by a rise in bond prices – directions for both of which are mentioned on the 6 o'clock news on TV.

SECURITIES: A general but posh-sounding term, which simply means any type of investment offered by a company or authority, which is usually also for sale to the general public, eg. shares, debentures, bonds, etc. are all different kinds of securities.

SECURITIES COMMISSION: The financial watch-dogs who keep an eye on the offering of *securities* in New Zealand, to ensure that everyone is playing by the rules, for example by making sure that investment offers come with a *prospectus* containing all the required information. The commission works with the stock exchange; can hold enquiries into *insider trading* allegations, and often issues warnings about pyramid schemes and other scams. To find out more about what the commission does, have a look at its website, www.sec-com.govt.nz.

SHARE (STOCK, STOCK UNIT): An equity (asset) which is also part ownership of a company.

SHARE PRICE INDEX: See *NZSE-50 index*.

SHORT POSITION: This happens when a trader sells securities he may not actually own yet. As a beginner, I would certainly hope you wouldn't attempt this! In 1709, the financial essayist, Joseph Addison, wrote an article for the London *Tatler*, likening short selling to 'selling the bear's skin before one has caught the bear'. However, the movie comedy *Trading Places*, starring Eddie Murphy and Dan Ackroyd, illustrates how some traders have made a lot of money with their skill and timing (albeit dubiously for the purposes of the comedy).

Handy hint

If the builder of your investment property says he's having trouble with product supply or quality from a company in which you're a shareholder, then check around to see if that's what other builders are experiencing as well. It could be a sign to sell your shares at the next best opportunity, before this fact is reflected in the next profit report and dividend.

Beware

Some major developers and home builders are now also major shareholders in companies which supply their building products. In my experience, this means they're not always choosing the best products for your home, but rather the products from which they get the most financial kickbacks and benefits. It also limits the number and type of variations or input you're permitted to have in the plans and construction — which is never a good recipe for maximising the capital growth of your investment property, if you choose to build your own.

SHARE SPLITTING: Sometimes a company might choose to adjust its capital issues by splitting its shares into units of lesser face value. Such splits of say $2 shares into 50 cent shares increase the number of shares in each portfolio and tend to make overall company shareholding more widespread.

SPECULATOR: Someone who buys shares with the hope of selling them very soon for a profit. L-plate investors are often scared out of investing in shares after attempting to be speculators before they are experienced enough to do it profitably. Therefore many of the anecdotes you hear about 'such and such' who lost money on the stockmarket, will be about speculators who should have left their L-plates on a little longer.

STAG: A person who applies for a new issue of securities (often through a prospectus) with the intention of selling immediately at a profit, as opposed to someone who invests for the mid- to long-term. I remember this snippet of jargon by imagining some poor groom who just bought into a brand new investment but has to dump his stocks soon after listing to pay for his stag party.

STOCKBROKER: See *broker*.

STOCK UNIT: It's a unit of capital, which is also another word for 'share'.

SYDNEY FUTURES EXCHANGE: This is where commodity and financial futures are traded, for New Zealand as well as Australia. There is potential for big profits fast, but greater risk of bigger losses faster for the uninitiated. For the L-plate investor, it's a nice place to visit, but you shouldn't want to stay there – certainly not before you have a thorough understanding of the market and are willing to give up plenty of your time every week to stay on top of it.

SUBSIDIARY: This is a company that is owned or controlled by another (but not necessarily bigger) company. Ownership or control doesn't have to be complete, but obviously it has to be by a majority in order to control voting.

T+3: This means Trade Date plus 3, meaning you've got three business days to pay up after you buy your shares. It also means you get paid within three business days after your shares were bought by someone else. In practice, most trades are settled within a day or so.

TAILGATING: When your broker slips in an order to buy or sell some of their own shares with your order, hoping to take advantage of the combined effect on the market. But it's illegal and not something that an L-plate investor can easily notice from their end.

TAKEOVER: When a company or group of individuals desires majority control (or a complete buyout) of an existing company, the bidder (potential buyer) will send letters to all shareholders inviting them to accept a certain price per share, usually by a certain date, often with the proviso that they get enough shareholders to accept their terms so they end up with the desired number of shares. Both friendly and hostile takeovers will involve letters from the company's existing directors to current shareholders too, and sometimes an advertising campaign for potential shareholders, which often plead, grovel and beg for the acceptance or rejection of the bidder's offer. You'll always know when there's a hostile takeover afoot because it will make the news and your letter from the directors will come with large bold and/or desperate type at the top. Either way, it makes

---

Handy hint

Before you fork out big bucks for that u-beaut stockmarket tracking analysis software that costs more than an inground swimming pool, with ducks, fountain and waterfall included, just imagine what 20,000 investors all using the same software will do to your share prices and opportunities.

you feel good to know you have the power over whether or not your directors get re-elected so they can afford a new Porsche next year.

THIN MARKET: Either where a share issue has only a limited number of shares available for sale, or where only a few buyers are available or interested, or a combination of both.

TREASURY BILLS: Short-term securities issued by the government through the Reserve Bank, for periods ranging from a month to a year and usually at a discount from their face value. The minimum investment required – a face value of $1 million – means these highly negotiable securities are usually the domain of professional investors. Only registered buyers can buy Treasury bills, which are sold by tender, usually once a week.

TRUSTS: This is where 'experts' manage a fund of 'pooled' investors' money from which investments are purchased and managed as a whole. Some trusts are diversified, with a variety of investments, while others specialise in one area. Three of the most common trust types are equity, property and cash management. Many seem to do really well for a while and then just lose the plot. Also, their definition of management fees often gets close to my definition of extortion. After reading this book I'd like to hope you'd be able to manage your own investments, with greater flexibility, satisfaction, control and profits, and without the added expense of a fund or trust manager. The mistakes or triumphs that you make – if any – will then be your own to learn from, profit by and brag about. Whereas if you commit to a long-term fund which eventually under-performs, you usually just have to cop it.

<u>UNDERWRITER:</u> Someone, usually a stockbroking firm but sometimes an accounting firm or other entity, which arranges a new issue of shares or other securities for a company, and which agrees to purchase any unsold securities in order to guarantee full subscription and therefore improve the chance of success for the listing.

Beware of stockbrokers who recommend purchasing shares in a floundering company in the first year after they've underwritten their launch onto the stockmarket, because they're probably just trying to release the cash they've got tied up in the venture – or worse, trying to ditch their dog stocks onto you.

UNIT TRUST: A syndicated form of investment where a manager invests funds on behalf of a group of investors. See also *trusts.*

UNSECURED NOTES: A loan made to a company for a fixed period of time at a fixed rate of interest, but it's not secured by a charge over any of the company's assets. Obtainable through your broker, it's like giving an unsecured personal loan to the company.

VANILLA PRODUCT: A straightforward, uncomplicated investment; for example, ordinary shares, fixed interest deposits and term accounts.

WARRANTS: Much like an option, a warrant gives the holder the right to buy a specific amount of the underlying securities or shares at a future date and is also tradeable by itself through your broker (unless it expires). Unlike options, however, warrants may not have expiry dates, which means you may sometimes hold the issuer to the terms of the contract indefinitely. Warrants come in many forms, with bizarre names like *naked, killer, diluted, wedding, privileged, put, bond* and *harmless* to name a few, so once you've got the hang of sharemarket investment and wish to stretch your strategies even further, contact your stockbroker for the latest information and availability for each.

WINDING UP: The cessation of business through a court order, or by a special resolution of creditors or shareholders. Assets must be sold up to pay out the liabilities and expenses of the business. See also *liquidator*.

WORKING CAPITAL: Current assets minus current liabilities.

XB, XD, XF, XI and XR: Occasionally you'll see these abbreviations for ex-bonus, ex-dividend, ex-offer, ex-interest and ex-rights, (in that order) where ex means 'without' in each case.

YIELD: This is the effective return to investors from a particular security, expressed as a percentage of the current market price. So shares with a nominal or par value of $2 may be reported to give a 10% dividend, but if the market is currently at $4 a share, then the dividend yield for current buyers will be only 5% if the same dividend is paid next time. See also *dividend rate* and *dividend yield*.

ZERO-SUM-GAME: A situation or stockmarket trade where an advantage to one party is a disadvantage to the other. For example, futures trading is a zero-sum-game because for every purchase there is a sale and for everyone who profits there is someone else making a loss.

Your happy ending

Excited? You should be. You now have the core of information all investors need before they make their first informed purchases in the stockmarket. Whether you pay an investment advisor to make your decisions for you, fork out big bucks on software and learning packages for yourself or, like me, prefer to DIY for annual returns of 30% to 70% (including high yield fully imputed dividends) for little or no cost, you'll no longer be leaving yourself wide open as a target for con-deals. Logic, basic maths and fundamental business skills can take you the rest of the way in designing your own system of investing. You can even choose to avoid the share-market and switch to property investments now – if you still feel that company part-ownerships are not the investment vehicle for you – safe in the knowledge that you're at least making your decision a more informed one, rather than just burying your head in the sand, out of fear. Remember, fear is a tool used by the big investors to drive timid investors to suit their own profits. Fight it.

Wherever you see the majority of investors swimming away from one type of investment towards another – currently, that's away from shares towards property – then look for the bargains in their wake and always remember that for every shareholder who sells out at a low price, someone else is buying to make a killing. Try grinning every time you hear the words market crash instead of frowning, and know that what it really means is buying opportunities for the traders in the know. That way, your investment future will be even brighter than ever.

Best of luck with it,
Anita Bell

Other finance books by Anita Bell

Your Mortgage is for people starting out with a clean slate.

Anita and Jim purchased and paid off their first home in three years on a combined income of under $50,000, when interest rates had soared to 17%. Here's all their hot tips and shortcuts so you can save decades and thousands too.

Your Money is for people who want to get and keep a clean slate.

Anita never realised just how differently she does things to everyone else until after her first book became a bestseller and people wrote to her asking for more of her favourite hot tips. So this book has tricks and short-cuts (for everything except your mortgage) and has a handy financial goal guide for everyone aged 14 and over. Also includes Anita's hot tips for better job resumes, saving thousands on cars, bank accounts, overseas holidays and more.

Your Investment Property is to help you maximise your profits from property.

Once you're on top of your existing financial situation, it's time to start getting ahead. Investment property is often the next step for many Kiwis and in this book, Anita shows you how to do it successfully. She'll guide you around the traps and help you through the tricks to make your investment a winner. You'll be tripling your returns in three years (or even less, just like Anita did).

Your Real Estate Jargon Explained.

A crash course on all the terms you're likely to come across in the property industry with definitions on what they can *really* mean. Also includes hot tips on tricks and traps so you can be alert when someone tries to sell you 'the best opportunity of your life'.

Additional notes pages for your convenience

Additional notes pages for your convenience

Additional notes pages for your convenience